What the Owls Know

What the Owls Know

Poems by

Paul Bernstein

© 2019 Paul Bernstein. All rights reserved.
This material may not be reproduced in any form, published,
reprinted, recorded, performed, broadcast,
rewritten or redistributed without
the explicit permission of Paul Bernstein.
All such actions are strictly prohibited by law.

Cover design: Shay Culligan

ISBN: 978-1-950462-10-0

Kelsay Books Inc.

kelsaybooks.com

502 S 1040 E, A119
American Fork, Utah 84003

Dedicated to the Memory of

Jerome Badanes

Friend and Mentor

Acknowledgments

The author gratefully acknowledges the following publications in which these poems first appeared.

The American Dissident: "Shadowfall"
Big River Poetry Review: "The Eye of the Storm," "The Anarchist Exiles at Geneva"
Blue Light Review: "Night Mares"
Creative Juices: "First Flight"
Drown in My Own Fears: "Prodigal"
Fourth and Sycamore: "A Day at the Races," "Heaven's Gate"
Freefall: "Locked In," "The Next World," "Worlds Apart"
Front Porch Review: "Dusk," "The Forecaster"
Glass Tesseract: "Sparrows"
Maelstrom: "My Piece of the Rock," "Treasure Chest"
Main Street Rag: "Day One of the Deluge," "Safe and Sound"
Magic Lantern: "First Encounter"
Muddy River Poetry Review: "Costume Party"
Napalm and Novocain: "Phototrope"
New Plains Review: "After Hours"
Number 1: "Christmas Lights"
Poesia: "Bed Spread," "Grandmother Teaches the Child About Death," "Skin Deep," "Words"
Poetry Quarterly: "The Withering Elms and I"
the new renaissance: "Sideshow"
Third Wednesday: "Chasing Shadows," "Footfall"
U.S. 1 Worksheets: "A Damned Shame," "A Prayer for the Departed," "First Date," "The Eye and the Ear," "The Pleasures of Old Men," "What the Owls Know" "Exiles"

The author is also indebted to Nancy Scott for her advice and support, to my beloved godson Derek, to my old friends Heather, Jon, and Louise, to Robert Sheff (aka "Blue" Gene Tyranny), and to Shireen, who woke me up.

Contents

Sideshow	11
What the Owls Know	12
Footfall	13
Prodigal	14
After Hours	15
A Prayer for the Departed	16
My Piece of the Rock	17
Bed Spread	18
The Years Fall Away With the Rain	19
Safe and Sound	20
Steps	21
Day One of the Deluge	22
The Forecaster	23
A Damned Shame	24
The Next World	25
Costume Party	26
Christmas Lights	27
Grandmother Teaches the Child about Death	28
Chasing Shadows: a Cinquain	29
Dusk: a Cinquain	30
Night Mares: a Cinquain	31
Daybreak: a Cinquain	32
Phototrope	33
Shadowfall	34
The Eye of the Storm	35
Close Encounter	36
Worlds Apart	37
Locked In	38
A Day at the Races	39
Treasure Chest	40
My Day and Yours	41
First Date	42
Skin Deep	43
The Ear and the Eye	44

The Eye and the Ear	45
Words	46
Paper Chase	47
Sparrows	48
First Flight	49
The Commuters	50
Exiles	51
The Pleasures of Old Men	52
The Anarchist Exiles at Geneva	53
Heaven's Gate	54
The Withering Elms and I	55

Sideshow

The sea climbs up to Coney Island
step by wrinkled step, drifting back
and forth on the beach
to the moon's beat, uncertain
of the promised land's hard comfort.

Gulls hobo up a thermal
swirled around the Thunderbolt's old bones
to ride the rails, scavenging down
the coaster's skeleton for scraps.

But it's winter now, the streets
are empty, everything's picked clean.

The Electric Ladies and the Giraffe-
Necked Women from Burma
still sashay up and down
Surf Avenue, searching in vain
for the long-lost rowdy boys
from the Navy Yard; their painted faces
flake off the woodwork sin by faded sin.

Even the barkers
have nothing left to say;
they huddle in trailers,
silent over coffee and smokes.

Only the Wonder Wheel still circles
heaven's houses high above the sideshow,
the empty beach, the climbing sea,
and the hungry, cold-eyed gulls.

What the Owls Know

Owls lurk in gloom
for ghosts to rise up
from their graves,
meet them and mate.
My people know that spirits
speak to us through owls,
hooting threats of sickness
and approaching doom.
They fear the owls
and do not speak of them.
But I was one of those who listen,
brooding on secrets
the dead alone can tell
until they hatch. So when owls
told me you were coming
my eyes grew big as plates
to search you out
and greet you friend to friend
in twilight, while owls rouse
themselves, stretch, strop
their beaks, and wait.

Footfall

The souls of trees are silent,
milky white and shy, rising
from heartwood to blink
between the elms like fireflies,
pricking the thickness of the night.
Crackled leaves beneath my feet
startle owls out of sleep
and spirits back to roots.

Prodigal

Pity the poor mother left
with a heartbreak of roses
while I, wild seed sprung
from her forsaken ground,
romp in the cowboy west.
Drunk on mescaline sunsets,
bar bands and the toxic
scent of women, I spilled myself
into careless girls to the clashing
beat of blues guitars and my
unanswered phone, unmoved
by a father's grave or mommy's
homeless love.

After Hours

Seared by the thick
red sorrow of sunsets,
I, stick-shape,
driven by jukeboxes,
sit beside somebody
else's woman, bonded
by the electric
communion of guitars.
The singer cups an ear
to catch the pitch;
his voice explodes,
backbeat stomp and rhythm
spin body to body,
twisting and winding
till the music ends
and silence unravels us
into our separate threads.

A Prayer for the Departed

Say a prayer
for Pluto, our distant
now demoted kin,
kicked out of heaven's
hierarchy, shrunk,
cast down into the heap
of old cold stones.
We humans know too much;
we kill off planets
with a show of hands
while our fearful universe
expands to anywhere it can,
leaving us diminished.
I for one will find
some broken place,
pour a libation mixed
of honey, blood and wine
down to the world's pit
where forgotten gods
lie thirsting for belief,
till their shadows thicken
and they complain
of old fool Prometheus
and his misbegotten
gift of fire.

My Piece of the Rock

Sisyphus had it easy
working his piece of the rock;
he had something to do,
muscling up to it, chest thumping,
fingers groped in cracks, back
braced against the weight.
The slab, shaken out
of sleep, climbs, rumbling,
greased in blood and sweat,
till gravity and Zeus take
their revenge and he can
only duck, or run like hell,
when the damned thing tumbles down.
Now me, I'm stuck with you,
a dead lump of stone
I can't move, that doesn't
care what I do or take
the trouble to roll over me.

Bed Spread

A thin slice of a girl
I picked up
buttered up and gulped,

a golden ring
I wore around my thighs;
the blonde

split, walked out,
fell back
to the simple streets.

I suppose
the circles of our lives
will swing around,

she will smile
her mouth
melting in my mouth.

The Years Fall Away With the Rain

My lost love
is back
with the rain.

The years
fall away as warm wet
beckons old seeds

back into belief,
shooting up new stalks
drenched

in foolish youth
and secret desperation
green again

Safe and Sound

I surrender my name
to the stranger who keeps
my kingdom's keys in trust
and grants me sanctuary.
The vault opens, promising
security beyond vows.
I've heard there's no such thing
as silence; in anechoic rooms
scrubbed clean of sound
the blood still rumbles,
the nerves tweet, cells go dancing
to the body's music. It's not so,
not here, I'm hushed all over.
A thin steel box is all I need
to hold a few sheets of verse
and a cold black stone
that was once was a heart.
Nothing's left for me but leaving.
Outside, life struts and clamors,
honking, bleeding secrets.
I strap and buckle,
turn the key, start the car,
bound and determined
to drive myself
all the way to the wedding.

Steps

Feet flat, arms flailing,
legs bowed from their confinement
in the womb, a child
struggles to heave himself
atop one wobbly limb.
He stumbles, falls, hurts.
Pain is the price he pays
for the first step.

We fall so many times
since the first fall from grace.
The world's weight
disputes our sinful bodies' progress
every step of the way.
We even fall in love,
too lost to stand up
to the world alone.

So here we are,
me chasing after you,
longing to be close.
Yes, I may stumble,
I may fall, I may come
crashing down to earth again.
Pain is the price I pay
each time my scarred-up
beaten-down believing bones
step into space.

Day One of the Deluge

Teacher called out duck
and cover, dropping me
behind my desk, H-bombs
raining down on me,
scared stiff, chicken little
in a broken shell
watching the sky fall.
That was second grade—I've kept
a wary eye on heaven ever since.
So don't ask me why
I'm out here ankle-deep in it
hawking umbrellas on day one
of the deluge, one eye cocked
on the Weather Channel.
Let the believers line up
two by two, waiting for the boat;
I'll tumble down with you, drowning
in pleasure, when the trumpet sounds
and the world's collected sins
lap enviously over me.

The Forecaster

Poor Cassandra prophesied
the fall of Troy, global warming,
and the housing bubble,
so everybody hates her,
she hasn't been kissed
for 2,000 years, and scrimps
for bread pitching forecasts
to the Weather Channel.
Now she's predicting
40 days and nights of rain,
and hangs out hopeless
on the corner crying,
hawking umbrellas,
grace, and meteorology
to believers blinded
by the faithless sun
that shines before the storm.

A Damned Shame

I matriculated in the Seven
Deadly Sins with a double major
in Sloth and Lust. Now I'm hung up
between languor and longing
with hard desire, clean sheets,
and a bewildered appetite.
So if I come on too strong
or not at all, be patient
while I sort my devils out.
And if I run around in circles
don't despair; for I, like you,
will get to hell in the end.

The Next World

When I got up to heaven
(to my surprise), God lit into me
for not believing till I spoke
your name. Now I'm saved
on satin sheets, waiting on Satan
to show you in (to your surprise),
for in the next world
grace will jumble up to justice
to lay on each of us the love
I lost and you deserve.

Costume Party

For Halloween I dressed up
as myself, molding foil
against my face, layering
paper dipped in paste,
dried and daubed
with paints, mascara,
blush and base to make
the mask a perfect me.
Wrinkled pants and shirt
a size too small, buttons
snapped, old black shoes
with broken heels, fused
into a mirrored mockery
of me to cast a pall across
the unsuspecting world
until my woman
looked, reflected, broke
the glass, seeing me
for what I was,
the way she does
every other day of my life.

Christmas Lights

Once a year I uproot
myself from city stones
to go to ground with you,
plunging out of solitude
into brash honking flocks
of boys migrating to manhood,
shedding old socks and mother love
along the way; aunts and uncles,
cousins, kids from anywhere;
a family fight, clattering, rude,
done with, quick as the snap
of a broken dish; and in morning
silence, the flash of a cardinal
through bare branches, the scratch
of squirrels crossing new snow
over dry leaves. This is what
the world is, what people do,
how children are, twinkling
bright as Christmas lights wound
around the stiff-branched, lopped-off
brooding tree invading house and home,
lending me light for one brief season.

Grandmother Teaches the Child about Death

Her mind fell like a leaf,
fading from red to gold
to wrinkled brown rot
eating up her breaking stem
until it cracked, and the wind
grew curious. A child listens
to her rasping breath. No one
taught him dying but grown-ups
whisper in the dark and weep,
he sees, he wants to know,
and aims his ripening wit
at grandma, to blow away
the wall between her life and his
and peek into the mystery.
This is not death, says the child,
there are no angels here,
no stink, not even silence,
and turns away
to the noisy comfort
of gunshots on the television.

Chasing Shadows: a Cinquain

Chasing
shadows, I pounce,
you flee, we laugh; two boys,
one bright, one dark, one live, one dead
escape.

Dusk: a Cinquain

Sunset
fades to shapeless
dark. The moon's black horses
stamp their hooves and whinny. A dream
awakes.

Night Mares: a Cinquain

I dreamed
I saw your face
in a posse of ghosts
chasing down life atop hope's wild
horses.

Daybreak: a Cinquain

Darkness
crumples into dawn.
Black horses, tossing manes,
trample sleep; moonset calls them home
untamed.

Phototrope

Daybreak. Emptiness
beside me, rumpled
and cold. Every day
begins in darkness.
Every night in dreams
I open up to you
too late and wilt
and wake up twisted,
a broken flower
searching in vain
for the morning sun.

Shadowfall

Life may be cheap but death
is pricey; the more we have
the less we can afford.
Our captains may count their prey
till the sky falls, but we little folk must pick
and choose in the charnel house
for a death we can wear,
a fitting death, one worth crying for.
So when you told me of the killing
of a kid a continent away I did not
care, but you knew him, wept
when I did not, raising up
this single unremembered death
to life for an accounting.
Now let me steal a little sorrow for myself.
Let the broken soul of the murdered boy
cast its ruined overarching grace
across the mystery between our life
and death the way that sunshine
turns to shadow in the afternoon;
a patch of dark come down
to make its way across our common ground
before the universal night.

The Eye of the Storm

for Anne Sexton

Shut the door. Block the pipe.
Turn the key and breathe.
It takes a while to die.
Was there, perhaps, a wisp
of time just long enough
for her to find peace
in the eye of the storm
that blew her life away?
Now only the words remain,
hard and bony, stripped
of flesh, hollow eyes
and bared teeth looming up
for us to marvel at; for a moment
we too escape and are eternal
till we close the book,
come up for air,
alive, breathless, safe.

Close Encounter

I never thought the slow
remorseless turning of the stars
could wind a mired soul
up root by root till ships
came singing out of space,
me trying to catch up,
a hunger for heights erupting
sharp and bright as a new tooth
in my mind's mouth.
I was invited, damn it,
invited all the way to heaven.
Then choppers came, and gas;
I fell, oh how we fell,
the unsuspecting birds and I
out of grace into this single
sinful old, unwelcome world.

In Steven Spielberg's Close Encounters of the Third Kind, *three characters reach the Devil's Tower. Two get to the top. The third never made it. This is his story.*

Worlds Apart

I've never been to California,
crossed the Rockies, climbed
high enough to catch the gleam
of mountain snow
shining back at the summer sky.
But my sleeping eye can
rake in universes, bend light
like a dying sun, punch a hole
in heaven deep enough to drag
the unsuspecting world and you
all the way down to me.
Oh, I can dream black dreams
and bold; it's the will that's weak,
a little stone without a star
drifting alone in the dark,
drowning in a teardrop.

Locked In

Locked in
they call it in the show
when a man
steps up to the plate and knows
that he can't miss.
The pitch comes in fat
and juicy, spinning madly,
trying to escape;
the wrists cock, the hips
unwind and for one perfect
time at bat
there's nothing to the game.

A Day at the Races

A racehorse is a mystery
incarnate in a miracle of grace
condemned to run around
in circles for the sake of sinners
lining up to lay out
all the faith they can afford.
The gates open, shouting colors
of the jockeys' shirts
kaleidoscope around the course
to the final judgment of the finish line.
We who prophesy in vain
can only pray in numbers
like Pythagoreans:
exacta trifecta quinella
hallelujah!! Amen.

Treasure Chest

We are all equals here, cooped up
in this box; let's keep our wits about us
and our tempers cool, no fights,
biting, scratching, beating
on our neighbors with impatient wings,
we have troubles enough.
The raucous sins that make the nightly news,
our common lusts and secret shames,
are also part of you or will be
when the lid comes off, it's what we do.
Till then let's get some sleep.
We will wake up when we hear
Pandora fumbling with the lock.

My Day and Yours

You'd like to know
about my day? My neighbors
want me gone, my wife
already left, old crow
Tiresias cawed at me
to find the hidden sin
and I did, at a fork
in the road, years back,
where the fool I whacked
turned out to be the dad
who wished me dead,
leaving me, Oedipus, king
and killer, family man,
with sisters for daughters
and mommy in my bed.
Now I'm supposed to claw
my eyes out, die homeless,
and wind up, so they tell me,
as a god. How was your day?

First Date

Cat curls herself
around my leg, flirts
her way into my lap.
My hands explore her body.
Her spine humps up;
teeth nip at fingers,
warning against liberties.
She's on her first date
with a boy she likes; curious
and careful, touching
but not to be touched
too soon, too fast,
today; not until tomorrow.

Skin Deep

Beauty is only skin deep, just enough
to tempt the snake I took into my bed;
It's a coat too confining to keep
I itch to get out of. Can you tell
I'm leaving? I think not.
So go ahead, fool, do what you please
with my empty shell, I don't care,
I'm hiding, coiled up tight,
hugging myself to myself
under a cold dead stone.

The Ear and the Eye

The smallest bones
make the loudest sound.
Hammer, anvil, stirrup,
drum beat out tunes
to woo the brain
and overwhelm the heart,
teaching us to dance,
marching us to war,
heating up the blood
of lovers. The eye
cannot do these things.
It can only watch.
That is why the eye
and not the ear
has to cry.

The Eye and the Ear

There is a path
between the eye and brain
the world can take
to overwhelm the heart.
The careless grace of birds
in flight, the swollen belly
of a starving child, a couple's
bumbling first embrace;
all this the eye records
or rejects, for while the ear
is always open the eye
can choose to see
or not to see, to cry
or to close.

Words

Nothing
but the world
and words

to make it sing
I snatched a woman's
heart, shaped it

into toys
of poems rattling
in my childish

hands until she broke.
The world
takes its revenge,

the woman lurches
out of love,
the poem's done.

Nothing left
but words
between us.

Paper Chase

I poured our hearts
onto a napkin for an old love
to keep; you drew a rift
between them crooked, black
and cold as our last night.
I sketched a stitch to heal
the split; you tore it up and left.
The scraps I tucked
into a memory to be recycled,
shredded, pulped and cleaned,
compacted, stacked up
at the bar again
with all the tattered
hopeful hearts condemned
to yet another pick-up,
stain and crumple.

Sparrows

I wake up to the sound of sparrows
bursting into flight, screeching
and hungry, murdering sleep,
so many damn birds all at once all over,
where do they hide?
I peep at building walls for sparrows
buried in brick deep as the white
blind birds trapped in tile
flapping up to the IRT at Dyckman Street
who never catch a train.
The sparrows do not ride, nor do they toil
to keep the timetables of their brief commute;
they are vagabonds, grimy and sly,
frolicking through shadow-dappled
climbing city stones like kids
tumbling into the streets
at the end of a lifelong day in school,
teaching us how children go to heaven—
in flocks, chattering, snatching for treats.

First Flight

I made a poem out of sparrows,
gulls and geese and cackling birds,
for me to speak and you to sing
when I released the caged words
flapping inside me, consonants
cawing like crows around the piping
coos, tweets, and chirps of the frightened
vowel sounds until the flock
took off to migrate all the way
to the kiss of your lips.

The Commuters

One sleepless night, stumbling
down subway steps, I found
an empty platform and a sparrow,
fallen from the sky
to this abandoned place,
fluttering from dark to dark, beam
to beam, lamp to broken lamp,
trying to escape. I do not know
how his commute or mine
will end; whether we are doomed
to wander aimlessly from stop to stop,
or if we both will finally take flight
from shadow into heaven's
cold uncertain light.

Exiles

Parrots
are psitticines
of the world,
but some birds,
like some men,
live out their lives
confined. My parrot
takes his revenge
bite by bite, snapping
buttons off my shirts,
stripping cable wires,
gnawing black holes
in the walls enclosing
his will and mine
in a crooked place
we were not made for,
forever inside looking out
at sun and stones, streets
and stars, and the endless
unbound sky.

The Pleasures of Old Men

Old men take what pleasures
they can, a patch of shade
on a sun-drenched day, a night's
uninterrupted sleep, a treasured
book, or food, or once-forgotten
name, or a young girl yawning
in the summer sun, her top
pulled upward rib by rib, bestowing
an unconscious gift of secret
warm unwrinkled skin.

The Anarchist Exiles at Geneva

Snow is falling again; it
drops out of the sky for no apparent reason,
the clouds dissolve, the snow
goes quietly about its business

and buries us. We never
hear it coming. It is too much
to understand, something to endure
in silence, our last bravery.

We have no martyrs now,
no one to mourn for;
we melt away slowly
beneath the stones with the snow.

There are many debates.
We read too much, and smoke.
The old men reminisce and die,
their eyes fixed on the mountains.

Heaven's Gate

I've served my three score
years and ten in full;
the bars are down,
gates open, heaven lurking
just outside the walls, but I
choose to linger
in the prison of the flesh
cell to cell with you
till my old body raptures
me to paradise, free
from guilt and sin and a life
locked up in righteousness
to reap my happy ending.

The Withering Elms and I

The wind awakes
the wasting artfulness of elms.
They brush the heavens
stroke them shyly into leafy green
and I am innocent again.

If like a child I choose
to paint the world to suit myself
till sun and sky collide,
tinting heaven to an emerald dream
then let me be.

For I am old; my limbs are brittle,
my trunk thick, but my roots still sip
the honeyed earth, my sap
still rises with the morning sun,

and I am free to toy
with words and worlds
bright and green as new spring leaves
unfolding from the withering elm.

About the Author

Paul Bernstein is a self-taught poet who began writing seriously after a varied career as a library worker/weekend hippie, anti-war activist, radical journalist, medical editor, and managing editor. His work now appears regularly in journals and anthologies. He is also a prizewinning amateur country music lyricist and a published photographer. Recent work has appeared or is forthcoming in *Front Porch Review, Muddy River Poetry Review, New Plains Review, Third Wednesday,* and *U.S. 1 Worksheets.* Paul currently lives in Ann Arbor, Michigan. He suffers from an addiction to Michigan sports contracted as an undergraduate but is otherwise functional.

www.ingramcontent.com/pod-product-compliance
Lightning Source LLC
Chambersburg PA
CBHW021027090426
42738CB00007B/933